Machine Learning for Predictive Maintenance
AI in Industrial Operations

Table of Contents

Chapter 1. Introduction

In this Special Report, we traverse the dynamic realm of machine learning and its vast applications in predictive maintenance, a phenomenon revolutionizing industrial operations. Bridging the chasm between the nitty-gritty and applicability, we delve into this tech-powered vista without the jargon overload. As we unfurl this rich tapestry, unpacking complex algorithms and enlightening strategies, you discover the immense potential of AI to predict and prevent machine failures, thereby enhancing operational efficiency and cost effectiveness. A must-read for anyone involved in Industrial Operations, this report promises to demystify the art of transforming raw data into actionable intelligence, making the future of manufacturing both exciting and accessible. So, if you're keen to explore this real-world synthesis of technology and industry, we invite you to gain insights and leverage the power of AI, minus the tech-heavy language, through our comprehensive Special Report.

Chapter 2. Unveiling Machine Learning: An Introduction

In the dynamic world of technology, it is machine learning that often takes center stage, driving unprecedented changes across myriad industries. This transformative technology, underpinning Artificial Intelligence (AI), offers powerful tools that help businesses 'predict' the future, revealing trends and patterns that can result in game-changing insights.

Let's uncloak the concept of machine learning, investigating its roots, principles, types, and how it appears in your everyday life, silently shaping workways and lifestyles alike.

2.1. Starting at the Roots - Where Machine Learning Begins

Machine learning has its roots in the profound field of mathematical statistics. Back in the 1950s, Alan Turing, a British mathematician, fertilized the thoughts of creating machines that could learn and evolve over time, just like any living organism.

Fast forward to the 21st century, and machine learning is a vital subset of the extensive AI domain now. To put simply, machine learning is a method applied to 'teach' computers to learn from data, recognize patterns, refine algorithms, and make predictions, all without human intervention.

2.2. The Foundation - What is Machine Learning, Really?

Machine learning revolves around algorithms - a set of rules or instructions given to computers. However, instead of explicitly programming for a task, machine learning algorithms adapt and improve their performance through experience, i.e., learning from a wealth of data. It's an attempt to mimic human learning, but at an incredibly faster rate with significantly increased accuracy.

The anatomy of machine learning encompasses patterns, features, models, and predictions, where features are attributes essential for prediction, and models are mathematical equations representing relationships among features.

2.3. Machine Learning in the Spotlight - Everyday Encounters

You may not realize it, but machine learning is abundantly present around you. From your silent digital assistant to the coveted recommendation engines on YouTube, Netflix, or Amazon, machine learning has empowered digital platforms to deliver personalized user experiences seamlessly. Other pragmatic realms of machine learning include predictive maintenance in industries, spam filtering in email inboxes, credit score predictions, facial recognition in security systems, and more.

2.4. Scratching the Surface - Types of Machine Learning

Machine learning primarily manifests itself in three types.

1. Supervised Learning - Herein, algorithms are well-guided with labeled input and output data, directing them towards accurate prediction. For instance, based on past data of confirmed spam emails (input) and their respective labels (spam or not-spam), a supervised learning model can accurately predict whether a new email is a spam or not.

2. Unsupervised Learning - This type involves exposing algorithms to unlabeled data and letting them 'discover' underlying structures or patterns on their own, just like a detective. It's helpful in exploratory analysis or when data labels are hard to obtain. Applications include segmentation of customers, dimension reduction, image compression etc.

3. Reinforcement Learning - A little unique from its cousins, reinforcement learning operates in an environment of 'trial and error.' It's like a game, where an agent takes actions in an environment to achieve a goal, and based on whether the action brings them closer to the goal, they're rewarded or punished. Over time, the agent learns to make better decisions to maximize rewards. An excellent example is a chess-playing AI.

2.5. Synthesizing Core Principles - How Machine Learning Works

The process of machine learning, naturally complex, comprises five notable steps: Gathering Data, Preprocessing, Choosing a Model, Training, and Evaluation.

1. Gathering Data - The first step involves collecting relevant and abundant data, which forms the foundation for machine learning. Data sources can hugely vary, including websites, sensors, databases, APIs, and more.

2. Preprocessing - This step involves data cleaning, normalization, and transformation, making it 'ready' for model training. It also includes dealing with missing or inconsistent data, removing outliers, and converting categorical data into numerical data.

3. Choosing a Model - Here, based on the type and nature of data as well as the problem at hand, an appropriate machine learning model is chosen. For instance, decision trees might be preferred for classification problems, while for numerical prediction, linear

regression might be a good fit.

4. Training - The chosen model is fed with the cleaned data, which it learns from. The training stage involves adjusting weights and biases to minimize error and enhance accuracy.

5. Evaluation - Finally, the model's performance is evaluated. Using metrics such as precision, recall, or area under the curve (AUC), the effectiveness of the model is assessed, tweaking the model if needed for better performance.

2.6. Why is Machine Learning Trending? - The Impact

Machine learning carries vast potential to transform industries and societies alike. By harnessing the power of automated learning, businesses can better predict trends, take proactive actions, and optimize efficiency. Whether it's predicting machine failures to schedule maintenance or providing personalized recommendations to customers, machine learning is a game-changer.

In conclusion, machine learning, deeply embedded with data, algorithms, and statistics, is steering the digital era into an intelligence era, where decisions are data-driven, machines are proactive, and businesses can unlock unforeseen avenues. Perhaps, the key takeaway is that machine learning isn't merely about understanding technology; it's about leveraging it to create valuable, actionable insights to drive innovation and growth, in ways we are only beginning to explore. As we progress in this report, we will delve deeper into its applications, especially in the realm of predictive maintenance.

Chapter 3. The Interplay of AI and Industrial Operations

AI has increasingly become an integral part of industry operations. Its element of predictive analysis assists in improving efficiency, accuracy, and effective decision-making. The intersection of AI and industrial operations offers a cornucopia of benefits, which we will delve deeper into this chapter.

3.1. The Role of AI in Industrial Operations

The application of advanced AI techniques to industrial operations has significantly revolutionized the sector. AI provides a conduit through which manufacturers can converge the physical and digital aspects of their operations. This confluence grants them the ability to exploit the power of advanced analytics to streamline their operations, improving output quality and operational efficiency. Implementation of AI within these operations also poses the promise of predictive maintenance, enabling managers to mitigate potential machine failure. This prevention in turn reduces costly unplanned downtime.

AI further improves operational efficiency through automation. Industrial operations can integrate AI with automation technologies such as Robotics Process Automation (RPA) to achieve speeds and seamlessness unattainable with human effort alone. AI has already engendered an evolution in many industry sectors, including manufacturing, logistics, and supply chain - changing how companies approach storage, delivery, and production.

3.2. Rise of Predictive Maintenance

Predictive maintenance has emerged as one of the key applications of AI in industrial operations. By utilizing machine learning algorithms, manufacturers can now anticipate and prevent equipment failures before they occur. The process involves utilizing machine learning to analyze data obtained from multiple sources, including sensors on the equipment, and predicting possible malfunctions.

Thereby, the system alerts the operator ahead of time, enabling preemptive action and reducing the probability of sudden machine halts. Predictive maintenance also eliminates unnecessary maintenance tasks, thereby extending the life of the machinery, and saving costs of replacement and repair.

3.3. Transforming Data into Actionable Insights

A significant way AI impacts industrial operations lies in its ability to turn raw data into actionable intelligence. In this context, AI extracts critical insights from big data - the vast amount of data generated in real time from various operations. Analyzing and making sense of this voluminous data is beyond human capability. Therefore, AI becomes instrumental in unveiling hidden patterns or correlations within the data, which can then be transformed into meaningful operational strategies.

Under the application of AI, big data transforms into predictive analytics, providing operators with potential scenarios and solutions, allowing for proactive, informed decision-making. This not only improves operational efficiency but also reduces risks associated with incorrect decision making.

3.4. The Promises and Challenges of AI in Industrial Operations

Despite the potential benefits, the implementation of AI in industrial operations comes with its share of challenges. Data privacy and security concerns are paramount. Adequate measures must be in place to protect sensitive data from leaking or falling into the wrong hands. Additionally, the integration of AI might lead to job displacements, as some roles could become redundant in the face of automation.

Nevertheless, the promises of AI in revolutionizing industrial operations far outweigh the challenges. By leveraging AI's efficiency, accuracy, and predictive capabilities, companies can boost productivity, reduce costs, and maintain a competitive edge in the ever-evolving industrial landscape.

To conclude, industrial operations are in the throes of an AI revolution. The dynamic capabilities of AI in predictive maintenance, data analysis, and automation are reshaping operational strategies and models. Imbuing industrial operations with AI is paving the way for a smart, efficient, and transformative future of manufacturing. Indeed, the interplay of AI and industrial operations is a reality that's here to stay.

Chapter 4. Infrastructure and Machine Learning: A Love Story

In the heart of industry, there is a bond developing that reshapes its landscape – a relationship between infrastructure and machine learning (ML). This remarkable partnership streamlines operations, enhances productivity, and increases reliability like never seen before. Built on a foundation of vast data pools and the ability to efficiently process this data, this union connects once isolated components, forging an intelligent network seldom experienced in the world of industrial operations.

4.1. The Bonding of Two Powerhouses

Infrastructure, the backbone of industry, has always been seen as a static, sturdy pillar, from heavy machinery to the assembly line. With time, however, these installations inevitably wear down, leading to unexpected machine failures, unscheduled downtime, and hefty expenses. This reality has propelled the search for proactive solutions, marking the expanded use of predictive technologies.

On the other hand, machine learning, an offshoot of artificial intelligence, grants profound insights into the behavior and life cycle of machines. With the ability to learn patterns and predict future circumstances without explicit programming, ML offers a solution to alleviate the downtime that plagues industrial operations.

The intertwining of infrastructure with machine learning is no accidental pairing but a purposeful union forged to boost efficiency and reliability within the industrial sector. The strength of infrastructure coupled with the predictive power of machine learning promises great potential for operational excellence.

4.2. Adaptive Algorithms: The Heart of Machine Learning

At the core of machine learning lie algorithms, sets of instructions that allow computers to learn from data. These rules simplify the detection of patterns, correlations, and anomalies in data – a crucial aspect of predictive maintenance.

Earlier models of predictive maintenance relied on pre-set rules for identifying component degradation. Such models had limited flexibility and could not adapt to the ever-changing operational conditions or the inherent variability in machinery. In contrast, machine learning algorithms continuously learn and adjust, growing in accuracy with each iteration.

While the types of machine learning algorithms are complex and countless, their integration into industrial infrastructure boils down to two main categories: supervised learning and unsupervised learning.

Supervised learning algorithms predict future occurrences based on past learnings. These algorithms need historical data, including fault occurrences and error data, to create predictive models. On the contrary, unsupervised learning algorithms discover hidden patterns and structures in data without guidance, detecting anomalies that could point to potential problems.

4.3. Infusing Machine Learning into Infrastructure

The integration of machine learning into industrial infrastructure begins with a thorough understanding of the physical system and a blueprinting of the mechanic and environmental conditions that could lead to failures.

Following this, data from the infrastructure is captured through sensors and other measurement devices, comprising various parameters such as temperature, pressure, vibration, and current. This raw data, a collection of numeric values, is processed and normalized to create informative datasets.

Subsequently, machine learning algorithms are then trained on these processed datasets. The training phase involves exposing the algorithm to historical data from which it learns to predict future situations. Once the algorithm is trained accurately, it's tested in a simulated or real-world environment and fine-tuned accordingly.

The final piece of the puzzle is implementing the trained algorithm into a dedicated platform. Here, the algorithm operates in tandem with the existing infrastructure, continuously monitoring, learning, and predicting possible anomalies. When the algorithm identifies a potential threat, it issues an alert, enabling operators to take corrective actions before the problem escalates.

4.4. The Industrial Revolution 4.0: A Love Story in Progress

The industrial revolution 4.0 centers around interconnectivity, automation, machine learning, and real-time data collection and analysis. In essence, it is a shift towards intelligent and connected systems.

The symbiosis of infrastructure and machine learning is emblematic of this revolution, showcasing the transformative power of marrying traditional industrial systems with advanced technology. Through predictive maintenance, machine learning increases the longevity of machines, decreases unscheduled downtime, and importantly, augments profitability.

This integration has been made possible by powerful computing technologies and the proliferation of big data. As more connected devices and systems pour into the industrial field, they produce exponentially more data. This data, unmanageable by traditional means, is the lifeblood for machine learning algorithms, equipping them to deliver accurate and timely predictions.

4.5. The Road Ahead

With the advent and maturation of Industry 4.0, the link between machine learning and infrastructure is only destined to grow stronger. Lessons learned from past deployments will further optimize machine learning algorithms, systems will become increasingly automated, and reliance on predictive maintenance will become a new industry standard.

In the long term, as machine learning evolves, it will uncover hidden efficiencies that current systems could never actualize. The bond with infrastructure will deepen, and together, they will write a love story that revolutionizes industry and its operations. This report aims to set the stage for this journey and invites you to explore this powerful alliance further.

Chapter 5. Decoding Predictive Maintenance: An Overview

Predictive maintenance, steered by the avant-garde force of Artificial Intelligence (AI) and machine learning, has emerged as a pivotal factor in the vast expanse of Industrial Operations. Put simply, predictive maintenance solutions powered by AI are shifting the maintenance paradigm from mere detection to out-and-out prediction.

5.1. Understanding the Essence of Predictive Maintenance

Predictive maintenance orbits around the concept of forecasting potential failure points in the manufacturing ecosystem, thus aiding in preventive measures. The collective ingenuity of AI and machine learning allows for the real-time monitoring of equipment and systems, leading to accurate predictions of possible breakdowns. The ideation behind this approach lies in minimizing unplanned downtime, safeguarding productivity and efficiency, and reducing maintenance costs. Predictive maintenance manifests the epitome of proactivity, with AI's mighty capability to learn from massive sets of data, discern patterns and anomalies, and predict outcomes with significantly high accuracy.

5.2. Technological Underpinnings of Predictive Maintenance

The tech base of predictive maintenance comprises of a threefold architecture: data collection, data analysis, and preemptive action.

Data collection is the first and crucial step, collecting information from various sources such as equipment sensors, operation logs, and environmental conditions. This data acts as a foundation to comprehend the behavior and performance of machines and systems.

Data analysis, the second tier, utilizes algorithmic models to analyze the collected data. Machine learning, along with advanced analytical methods, helps in identifying patterns and gaining insights into potential system inefficiencies or faults.

Preemptive action, the final tier, involves notifying the concerned managers or operators about potential risks identified through the analysis. With this information, preventative measures can be taken before a failure transpires, averting costly downtime and enhancing operational efficiency.

5.3. Machine Learning: A Key Enabler

Machine learning, a subset of AI, is the locomotive driving predictive maintenance. It enables machines to learn from past data, understand patterns, adapt to new scenarios, and predict future outcomes, all with minimal human intervention.

The process begins with training the model on historic data to identify meaningful patterns. These patterns form the basis of the machine learning model's 'knowledge' and are used to predict future failures effectively.

Machine Learning techniques in predictive maintenance include Supervised Learning, Unsupervised Learning, and Reinforcement Learning, each having its peculiar significance and application.

5.4. Role of Sensors and IoT in Predictive Maintenance

Weaved into the fabric of predictive maintenance are sensors and IoT (Internet of Things) devices. These enable real-time monitoring and feed data to AI and machine learning models for execution. From temperature and pressure readouts to vibration levels and energy consumption, an array of measurable parameters provide a holistic picture of machinery health. IoT devices harvest this data, over which the models train, and eventually lead to more reliable, efficient operations.

5.5. Building a Predictive Maintenance Model: A Step-by-Step Process

Initiating a predictive maintenance model involves an exhaustive multi-tiered process:

1. Define Goals: Determine what machinery or systems could benefit from predictive maintenance. Recognize what failures you aim to predict.

2. Data Collection: Gather data from relevant equipment using sensors and IoT devices.

3. Data Cleanup: Cleanse and format the data to make it suitable for analysis.

4. Select the Right Machine Learning model: Use the suitable machine learning model for prediction – Regression, Classification, Clustering, etc.

5. Training and Validation: Train the machine learning model using a supervised or unsupervised approach, validate its efficacy.

6. Test the Model: Test the model with real-time data to gauge performance.

7. Deployment and Improvement: Deploy the predictive model and monitor its performance. Iterate and modify accordingly.

5.6. Industry-Specific Applications of Predictive Maintenance

Over the past decade, many industry sectors have been harnessed the transformative power of predictive maintenance including Aerospace, Energy, Healthcare, and Automotive, amongst others.

In Aerospace, predictive maintenance can foresee factors causing ground time, thereby allowing preemptive actions. In the energy sector, it can minimize the risk of sudden equipment failure thereby ensuring continuous power distribution. In healthcare, hospitals employ predictive maintenance to reduce downtime of critical equipment, such as MRI machines, enhancing patient care. The automotive industry uses predictive maintenance to optimize production lines, maximize vehicle reliability, and foster the phenomenon of 'smart factories'.

Predictive maintenance, fortified by AI and machine learning, is redefining the operational landscape across diverse industries. It is no longer a distant concept, but a robust, tangible solution that is transforming our world, accelerating progress and reinforcing robustness in systems that we rely on.

5.7. The Road Ahead

The journey of predictive maintenance is only at its beginning. As machine learning models continue to improve and more high-quality, real-time data becomes available, the predictive accuracy will only increase, and its applications will become even more diverse. One can anticipate a future where predictive maintenance, coupled with AI, is the norm for a vast array of systems and infrastructure. Rapid technological advancements are pushing the boundaries of what is possible, turning today's explorations into tomorrow's realities.

In conclusion, this vibrant realm of predictive maintenance is a promising horizon for progress and efficacy. Its interplay with AI and machine learning is arguably the game-changer for industries worldwide, equipping them towards seamless operations with reduced downtime, better efficiency, and enhanced cost effectiveness. Harnessing its power will separate the leaders from the rest in the competitive arena of industrial operations.

Chapter 6. Data Collection and Preprocessing: The First Step

The foundation of machine learning and predictive maintenance lies in robust data collection and preprocessing practices. This initial step has the power to optimize or curtail the very outcomes algorithm crunching yields. Gathering data from various sources and processing it in a way that it can be utilized effectively are paramount tasks. Without appropriate preprocessing, hoards of data bear little to no value, rendering them a gratuitous heap of unstructured information.

6.1. Data Collection: The Underpinning of Predictive Maintenance

Data collection forms the backbone of any machine learning algorithm. In the context of predictive maintenance, the sources are generally machines or equipment. The types of data that can be collected largely fall into two categories: the first is data generated from the machine's internal sensors, such as temperature readings, vibration levels, and error codes. The second category is data which isn't explicitly generated by the machine, but instead reflects its operating conditions, such as ambient temperature, usage hours, load, and external environmental conditions.

Facilities are increasingly adopting connected machinery with Internet of Things (IoT) capabilities, which generate voluminous time-series data. This data can be used to track and predict the health status of industrial machinery, but also presents a new challenge of managing big-data. Nevertheless, this pool of data serves as an invaluable resource for digesting and discerning patterns that preclude imminent equipment failure.

Other sources of tend to be static data, such as machine type, its age, and maintenance history. Capturing this data can offer remarkable insights into the correlation between a machine's age, usage, and the likelihood of system malfunctions - data that is crucial in predicting machine failures.

6.2. Preprocessing: Organizing the Chaos

Even the most comprehensive data collection strategies would be rendered redundant without the second crucial aspect of this first step - preprocessing. The raw data collected from machines is invariably diverse and unstructured. It is through preprocessing that this raw data is transformed into a structured format that can be digested by machine learning algorithms.

A primary task in preprocessing is dealing with missing data. In the ideal world, every sensor reading would be taken at a consistent interval without fail, but factors such as sensor malfunctions or network headaches can cause gaps. This irregularity needs compensation by imputation methods, maintenance of algorithms that can handle missing data or simply by discarding the incomplete records.

6.3. The Clean Up Act: Data Cleansing

Data cleansing is a key preprocessing task that ensures the reliability of machine learning models. This stage of preprocessing involves removing duplicate entries, fixing structural errors, and eliminating any irrelevant observations that might skew the subsequent analysis. Cleansing may also entail handling outliers - these could be sensor malfunctions or valid anomalies, and have to be dealt with accordingly to maintain optimal accuracy during subsequent stages.

6.4. Harmonizing Heterogeneity: Data Integration

In an industrial setup, data often comes from disparate sources. These sources can be varied, producing data in different formats, scales, and units. Thus, data integration is a pivotal substep in preprocessing. Here, data from differing sources is combined into a unified format and represented in a way that facilitates subsequent machine learning operations. Data normalization often forms a part of this step, effectively scaling different data types to comparable ranges, allowing effective application of machine learning algorithms.

6.5. The Finer Nuances: Feature Engineering

Feature engineering fiddles with the finer details. Here, new features are created from the raw data that will allow the machine learning models to better understand the patterns within the data. This might involve creating composite features from multiple data points, such as a moving average taken over a specific window of time. The right set of features can drastically escalate the accuracy of predictive maintenance models.

6.6. Building a Predictive Powerhouse: Data Dimensionality Reduction

Finally, data dimensionality reduction is a powerful process that eliminates irrelevant features, improves model performance, reduces overfitting, and diminishes computational requirements. Techniques such as Principal Component Analysis (PCA) can be used to reduce dimensions of the data set, making sure the model focuses only on what's crucial to predict machine failures.

To conclude, understanding the synergy between data collection and preprocessing is the cornerstone of setting effective AI algorithms in action. By tenaciously trawling through diverse data, rigorously refining it, and then coherently framing it in a structured mold, we initiate the creation of intelligent models which help predict and prevent machine failures.

Chapter 7. Applying Machine Learning Models for Predictive Maintenance

The myriad applications of machine learning (ML) are rippling across various industries, with predictive maintenance standing as a prime example. The pattern recognition potential of ML can seamlessly decode anomalies in typical machine functions, forecasting potential failures and unlocking a new spectrum of cost and efficiency benefits.

7.1. Mechanics of Predictive Maintenance

Central to understanding how machine learning ushers in these benefits is a basic comprehension of predictive maintenance. Conventionally, industries relied on routine or reactive maintenance models. Routine maintenance involved scheduled checks while reactive maintenance was a knee-jerk response to machine breakdowns. These approaches, while straightforward, often generated hefty repair costs and unexpected downtime.

ML-powered predictive maintenance, on the other hand, centers on forecasting potential machine failures, adopting preemptive measures to prevent them. Before we detail how ML facilitates this, let's explore some key components of predictive maintenance:

1. Monitoring: The first step is keeping tabs on the operational data of the machines. These can be straightforward metrics like temperature or pressure, or more complex readings such as vibration patterns.

2. Comparison Analysis: The collected data is continually compared

against pre-defined standard benchmarks. Any deviations from the normal parameters can indicate potential failures.

3. Analysis and Predictions: This is where ML steps in. By recognizing patterns in the plethora of incoming data, predictive models can identify anomalies, predict possible failures, and suggest appropriate interventions.

Remember, the actionable intelligence hinges on the quality and consistency of the data. Clean, well-structured data feeding the system ensures reliable results.

7.2. Types of Machine Learning Models

Predictive maintenance deploys a range of ML models. Let's unpack a few of these to understand their specific benefits:

1. Regression Models: Regression is a statistical method used for predicting a dependent variable based on one or more independent variables. In the context of predictive maintenance, regression models typically predict one of two things – the Remaining Useful Life (RUL) of a machine, or the Time To Failure (TTF).

2. Classification Models: In contrast, classification models are intended to categorize data into predetermined categories. For predictive maintenance, these models will usually predict whether a machine failure is imminent within a specific period.

3. Time Series Analysis: These are especially useful in predictive maintenance as they treat time as a crucial factor. With this method, patterns are detected based on temporal changes, providing an extra layer of precision that feeds significantly in preventive strategies.

7.3. Building and Deploying Machine Learning Models

Having understood the types of ML models, we'll now dive into the steps involved in the creation and deployment of these models. This process is common across most ML models used for predictive maintenance:

1. Data Collection: As earlier mentioned, quality data is the backbone of ML. Thus, the first step always involves gathering accurate operational data from the machines. These could be sensor readings like temperature, pressure, vibration, etc.

2. Data Preprocessing: This stage deals with cleaning the data, managing missing values, reducing dimensionality, and ensuring the data is in the right format for the ML models.

3. Model Selection: Based on the specifics of the maintenance goal, you need to identify the right ML model. Remember, each model type has unique strengths and best-fit scenarios.

4. Model Training: Once you've selected your model, the next step is to feed it with a portion of your preprocessed data. This training helps the model to learn and identify patterns.

5. Model Testing: The model gets tested with a different section of the preprocessed data that was not used during the training. If the model's predictions align with the actual output, your model is deemed efficient.

6. Deployment: The final step of the journey is deploying the successfully trained model on the actual machines for live predictions.

Indeed, the application of machine learning models for predictive maintenance is revolutionizing industrial operations. From predicting machine failures to optimizing costs and enhancing operational efficiency, the transformative potential of AI is bringing the future of manufacturing within reach. With quality data and the right models, any industry can tap into this potential and ride the crest of this tech-powered wave.

Chapter 8. Fine-tuning and Model Optimization for Ideal Outcomes

Machine learning models are rarely perfect right out of the box. Practical implementation demands the honing and refinement of these models to ensure they deliver optimal results in predictive maintenance. This process is a combination of fine-tuning and optimization steps aimed at bolstering the performance of models, enabling them to zero in on anomalies and predict machine failures more accurately.

8.1. Building a Baseline Model

Starting with a baseline model is crucial for fine-tuning and optimization exercises. Here, the choice is often a simple machine learning model that fits the data and problem type. This baseline serves as the benchmark for gauging the performance of more sophisticated models. It provides insights on what level of accuracy or precision can be achieved without any stringent optimization and acts as a yardstick to measure the improvements.

8.2. Choosing the Right Algorithm

Determining the most effective algorithm is a significant – and often daunting – step in the model optimization process. Practitioners leverage a variety of machine learning algorithms such as Decision Trees, Random Forest, Support Vector Machines, and Neural Networks, depending on specific circumstance and requirements. The key determinant here is the nature of the problem – is it a classification problem, regression, or something else?

Machine Learning experts often rely on prior experience or heuristics to select the right algorithm. What works wonder in one case might falter in another. This choice influences performance and should therefore be deliberate and informed.

8.3. Model Hyperparameter Tuning

Every machine learning model is defined by a set of parameters. Hyperparameters form the upper level of these parameters, guiding how the model's algorithms learn from the data. Examples of hyperparameters include the learning rate in a gradient descent or the depth of a decision tree. Their values are not learned from the data but are set a priori.

Model hyperparameter tuning requires adjusting these settings with the aim of optimizing your model. Grid search, random search, and Bayesian optimization are common strategies used in this process.

Grid search systematically works through multiple combinations of parameter tunes, cross-validating as it goes to determine which tune gives the best performance. Random search, on the other hand, selects random combinations to perform the same operation, yielding similarly effective results but often in a more time-efficient manner. Bayesian optimization functions differently, building a probability model of the objective function to find the global optimum.

Choosing one of these techniques depends largely on available computational resources, model complexity, and dataset size.

8.4. Feature Engineering

In machine learning, relevance of features matters significantly in training a model achieving high performance. Feature engineering involves selecting the most useful features – or creating new ones – to improve model performance.

Many times, the raw data collected is not immediately suitable for feeding to the machine learning model. Data might need to be normalized or standardized, categorical variables could require transformation into numerical values, missing data needs addressing, or new features might have to be engineered from existing ones to enhance the model's predictive power.

8.5. Handling Overfitting and Underfitting

Model optimization is not just about achieving high performance. Striking the right balance between bias (underfitting) and variance (overfitting) is equally vital to ensure that the model generalizes well to unseen data.

Regularization techniques such as L1 and L2 are commonly employed to manage overfitting. These methods add a penalty term to the loss function, thereby discouraging the model from learning overly complex patterns – a common contributor to overfitting.

For underfitting problems, options include increasing model complexity, boosting features, or using ensemble methods such as bagging or boosting to improve performance.

To ensure both these issues are addressed, it's advised to keep a separate validation set to monitor the model's performance and make adjustments as needed.

8.6. Evaluation and Iterative Optimization

Evaluation and iterative optimization is the final stage, where the model's performance is continuously monitored and iteratively optimized for ideal outcomes. Analysing how the model works on a test set (unseen data) can provide a rough measure of how it will perform in the real world.

There are various evaluation metrics available, the choice of which depends again on the nature of the problem – is it a regression, classification, or clustering problem?

Common metrics include accuracy, precision, recall, ROC AUC for classification problems; mean absolute error, mean squared error, or R squared for regression problems; and silhouette score or Davies–Bouldin index for clustering problems.

Such an iterative approach to fine-tuning and optimization allows for the continuous enhancement of the model's performance over time, ensuring that the predictive maintenance program becomes ever more efficient and effective.

In conclusion, fine-tuning and model optimization for ideal outcomes in predictive maintenance involves an artful blend of several iterative, strategic decisions and underlying technical nuances. Each step plays a crucial role, shaping the efficacy of the machine learning model to predict and prevent machine failures, enhance operational efficiency, and reduce costs – truly unlocking the immense potential of AI in industrial operations.

Chapter 9. Case Studies: Success Stories from the Field

Innovations in machine learning is fostering a new era of industrial operations, characterized by increased accuracy, reduced downtime, and cost savings. Herein, we take a look at some substantial case studies that reflect the transformation brought about by predictive maintenance in various sectors of industry.

9.1. Predictive Maintenance in Aviation: An Airbus Success

Airbus, one of the leading players in the aerospace industry has brilliantly leveraged predictive maintenance. They embraced an approach called Prognostics Health Management (PHM) which relies on machine learning algorithms to detect abnormal behaviors and predict future ones using historical data.

In one illustrative case, sensors were installed throughout their aircrafts to monitor component behaviors. These sensors produced a vast amount of data each hour, which was then analyzed by machine learning algorithms. The results were impressive: The model detected and predicted component failures with high accuracy, which helped Airbus reduce unscheduled maintenance and improve operational efficiency.

What singled out Airbus's success was assuming a comprehensive perspective. Airbus didn't just focus on predictive maintenance: the company transformed its entire operational process, enabling engineers, technicians and managerial staff to work seamlessly in the data-rich environment.

9.2. Revolutionizing Pharma with Predictive Maintenance: The Merck Story

In the pharmaceutical industry, Merck, a global healthcare company, embraced predictive maintenance to enhance production efficiency. Known for their strategic use of data, Merck utilized machine learning to predict and prevent equipment failures in their processing plants.

The prime focus was on creating a predictive model capable of anticipating the breakdown of essential components. Machine learning algorithms analyzed enormous volumes of historical and real-time sensor data from equipment across various plants. Over time, the model bolstered its prediction accuracy, considerably reducing unplanned downtime and amplifying operational effectiveness.

Apart from these operational benefits, predictive maintenance afforded Merck substantial cost savings. Labor costs plummeted due to fewer repair needs while replacement costs also declined because parts were replaced only when necessary.

9.3. Harnessing Predictive Power in Energy: RWE's Pioneering Journey

RWE Generation SE, a leading international electricity and gas company, also joined the predictive maintenance bandwagon and transformed their energy production process. Focused on coal, nuclear, gas, and renewable energy production, RWE developed an AI model to predict potential malfunctions in their power production plants.

Data from thousands of sensors installed on their machines was fed into a predictive algorithm. The AI model they developed forecasted equipment malfunctions days before they occurred, allowing RWE to schedule maintenance more effectively.

In doing so, RWE was able to minimize the gap between energy production and distribution, maintain a steady stream of power for consumers, and increase their operational efficiency by leaps and bounds.

The incredible journey of these industry-leaders serve to showcase the transformative power of predictive maintenance. The potential of AI to analyze complex data and provide clear, actionable insights is becoming central to the future of manufacturing and industry.

These riveting case studies not only reflect predictive maintenance's transformative potential, but also demonstrate the versatility of AI implementation across distinct sectors. What makes predictive maintenance an ideal application of machine learning is its flexibility in fitting into different operational models and an array of industry sectors. It's more than a technological tool; it's a game-changing strategy that stands to redefine the way industries operate in the future.

In the unfolding landscape of industrial evolution, the agile implementation of predictive maintenance is more than an innovation—it's a call to action. As we move ahead, we invite you to join an exploration of the methods and processes underpinning this revolution. Together, let's understand how machine learning algorithms, when made comprehensible and accessible, can unfurl a future of unprecedented operational efficiency and industrial reinvention.

Thus, success from the field beckons organizations across sectors to embrace predictive maintenance. The immediate and long-term rewards of implementation are tangible and impactful—increased efficiency, reduced costs, and enhanced decision-making. Predictive maintenance, powered by AI, is poised to be the cornerstone of the Industry 4.0 era. This report is a testament to the possibilities and proven impact that stand before every industry on the brink of AI-infused transformation.

Chapter 10. Confronting Challenges: Risks and Remedies

The exciting quest to apply machine learning for predictive maintenance does not come without its hurdles. Several potential challenges might arise when implementing predictive maintenance algorithms, along with associated risks. However, each issue presents an opportunity for finding remedies and improving systems, ultimately leading to superior performance and a more nuanced understanding of this technology's potential.

10.1. Identifying Warning Signs

The first issue at stake in predictive maintenance is the need to comprehend the signals or warning signs emitted by a machinery that predict upcoming failure. This task involves understanding raw data generated by IoT-enabled sensors and tools, recognizing patterns and anomalies that signify malfunctions.

While the notion of identifying patterns may seem straightforward, remember that we are dealing with expansive amounts of data, in different formats such as images, sensor readings or vibration data from thousands of sensors. This rich dataset is a double-edged sword; while necessary for accurate predictions, the sheer volume can complicate analytics and dilute valuable insights.

Remedying this challenge involves optimizing data collection processes and refining algorithms, aiming to mine only the most significant and revealing data. This approach, known as feature selection, ensures resources are used to analyze the most valuable information. Another strategy would involve integrating machine learning algorithms that can efficiently process unstructured data, enabling the extraction of insights from diverse data sets.

10.2. Addressing Data Quality and Accuracy

Data quality directly impacts the accuracy of predictive maintenance models. Flawed or incomplete data can lead to incorrect or unsatisfactory model predictions. Inaccurate data can occur due to faulty sensors, connection glitches, inadequate data capture methods, or even human errors during manual data entry.

To mitigate these risks, companies must invest in the quality control of their data collection methods. Regular maintenance and calibration of sensors are necessary to ensure reliable data. In addition, rigorous data cleaning processes, bearing in mind specific industry requirements and machine characteristics, should be implemented to enhance data accuracy and integrity.

10.3. Managing Resource Constraints

Resource constraints also pose significant challenges. Implementing predictive maintenance, in some contexts, would require an overhaul of current maintenance systems, which can demand significant capital investment and time.

To overcome this obstacle, a phased approach can be beneficial. Starting with smaller projects and progressively scaling them across the organization can gradually realize the benefits while better managing resource allocation. Additionally, utilizing cloud-based machine learning platforms can alleviate concerns related to computing power and storage, thereby enabling a smoother transition towards predictive maintenance.

10.4. Navigating Regulatory Requirements

Sometimes, the use of AI-driven predictive maintenance can potentially run afoul of regulatory guidelines, particularly in industries like healthcare or aviation, where safety is paramount. Predictive algorithms will need to prove reliability before gaining acceptance in such sectors.

Organization must develop robust compliance strategies, integrating legal and cybersecurity standards into the design of predictive maintenance systems. They should also stay abreast of regulatory changes to ensure the legal use of AI technologies in their specific industry context.

10.5. Cultural Resistance to AI Adoption

Another potential obstacle is the cultural resistance to adopting new AI-based tools within an organization. Employees could exhibit apprehension towards technology that appears to threaten their jobs and change established work routines.

Managing this change requires careful strategizing. Clear internal communication about the benefits of AI, education about how these tools will augment rather than replace human roles, and training programs to upskill workers can enable smoother integration of AI-based predictive maintenance.

In sum, it's clear that the pathway to implementing machine learning in predictive maintenance is fraught with challenges. However, it's equally clear that these challenges—all surmountable—can serve as stepping stones towards designing robust systems. By identifying and addressing these risks head-on, businesses can achieve the twin advantages of machine efficiency and cost rationalization that predictive maintenance promises.

Chapter 11. The Future: Trends and Opportunities in Predictive Maintenance

As the curtain ascends on the new era of Industry 4.0, machine learning-based predictive maintenance emerges as a leading protagonist, poised to rewrite the script of industrial operations. Rare is the trend that combines the promise of significant economic payoff with a radical shift in the operational paradigm, setting the stage for a host of opportunities yet unexplored.

11.1. The Paradigm Shift to Predictive Maintenance

Advancements in machine learning and AI have reshaped our approach to equipment maintenance. The traditional practice of prescheduled "preventive" maintenance, siloed and devoid of real-time insights, is no longer adequate for today's interconnected industrial world. In contrast, predictive maintenance offers compelling advantages.

Leveraging the power of machine learning algorithms, predictive maintenance utilises the continuous flow of data from machine sensors to anticipate potential breakdowns, allowing for timely interventions and avoiding costly downtime. This shift from reactive to proactive management has impressive implications for the operational efficiency, reliability, and life cycle of machinery.

11.2. Machine Learning: The Heart of Predictive Maintenance

Unearthing the treasure trove of data collected by sensors embedded in modern machinery, machine learning models pave the way for insightful decision-making. By applying tools such as classification, regression, and anomaly detection, these models discern patterns in the data, predicting possible anomalies before they escalate into failures.

However, one size does not fit all; the success of predictive maintenance hinges on identifying the right machine learning model that best fits your unique operational context. While regression models are praised for their finesse in gauging remaining useful life, classification techniques excel in predicting failure occurrences. Moreover, unsupervised learning algorithms, particularly anomaly detection, bring a fresh perspective by identifying rare events that are often the precursors of significant failures.

11.3. The Twin Pillars of Predictive Maintenance: IoT and Cloud Computing

The advent of the Internet of Things (IoT) and cloud computing technology has fueled the surge in predictive maintenance. IoT devices, ranging from vibration sensors to temperature sensors, serve as the eyes and ears of the system, capturing crucial data in real-time. This massive data flow is then channelled to cloud platforms, where it's processed and analysed by machine learning models. The cloud's scalability, coupled with its massive computing power, turns the dream of real-time predictive maintenance into a practical reality.

11.4. Big Data Analytics: Powering Insights

Big data analytics is a crucial component in the predictive maintenance ecosystem. It transforms the raw sensor data into digestible insights that trigger actions, whether that means scheduling maintenance or averting an imminent machine failure. Armed with these insights, decision-makers can optimise operations, reduce unnecessary expenditure, and improve overall productivity.

11.5. The Dawn of Digital Twins

Digital Twin technology, the virtual replicas of physical systems, is a major game changer in predictive maintenance. By mirroring real-world machinery, digital twins facilitate detailed scrutiny of the systems under various operating conditions. The fascinating interplay of digital twins with AI and machine learning allows for the prediction of breakdowns, thereby enhancing the system's reliability and longevity.

11.6. The Role of Cybersecurity in Predictive Maintenance

As we plug into the connected world of IoT and predictive maintenance, cybersecurity grows into a paramount consideration. The convergence of operational technology with information technology exposes vulnerabilities that hackers can exploit — making robust, multilayered cybersecurity measures essential.

11.7. The Future of Predictive Maintenance: A Thematic Overview

Looking to the future, a few themes stand out in the world of predictive maintenance:

- Autonomization and Artificial Intelligence: Predictive maintenance is getting smarter, gradually moving towards full autonomization. AI-driven systems will be capable of self-diagnostics and repair, revolutionizing maintenance procedures.

- Edge Computing: As real-time data processing becomes vital, edge computing comes into the picture. It brings data processing closer to the source, speeding up response times and enhancing predictive capabilities.

- The Robots are Coming: Robots, especially drones, will play an increased role in predictive maintenance, especially in inaccessible areas, augmenting human capacities and enhancing safety measures.

- 5G and Improved Connectivity: With the increased demand for high-speed connectivity for real-time data processing, the role of 5G in predictive maintenance is set to expand.

As predictive maintenance continues to mature, the industrial sector must prepare to ride the wave of this revolution. The opportunities and efficiencies it brings are worth pursuing. It's imperative to remain informed, adaptable, and innovative to fully harness the benefits of this transformative trend.

www.ingramcontent.com/pod-product-compliance
Lightning Source LLC
Chambersburg PA
CBHW071555080326
40690CB00057B/2629